# FUN FABRICS

by Ruth Owen

**PowerKiDS** press.

New York

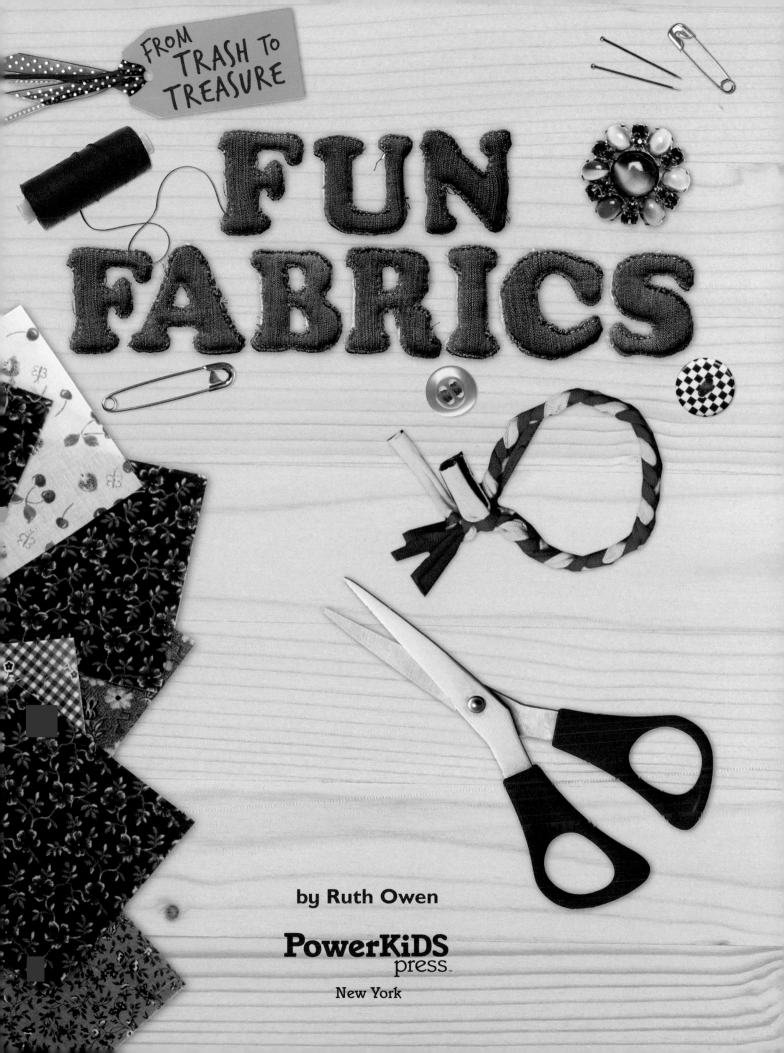

Published in 2014 by The Rosen Publishing Group, Inc.
29 East 21st Street, New York, NY 10010

First Edition

Produced for Rosen by Ruby Tuesday Books Ltd
Editor for Ruby Tuesday Books Ltd: Mark J. Sachner
US Editor: Joshua Shadowens
Designer: Emma Randall

Photo Credits:
Cover, 1, 3, 4–5, 6 (left), 7 (top), 13 (bottom right), 14 (left), 22 (bottom) © Shutterstock; cover, 1, 6 (right), 7 (bottom), 8–9, 10–11, 12–13, 14 (right), 15, 16–17, 18–19, 20–21, 22 (top), 23, 24–25, 26–27, 28–29, 30–31 © Ruth Owen and John Such.

Library of Congress Cataloging-in-Publication Data

Owen, Ruth, 1967–
 Fun fabrics / by Ruth Owen. — First edition.
    pages cm. —  (From trash to treasure)
 Includes index.
 ISBN 978-1-4777-1284-9 (library binding) — ISBN 978-1-4777-1362-4 (paperback) — ISBN 978-1-4777-1363-1 (6-pack)
 1. Textile crafts—Juvenile literature. 2. Recycling (Waste, etc.)—Juvenile literature. I. Title.
 TT699.O94 2014
 745.5—dc23

                             2013010458

Manufactured in the United States of America

CPSIA Compliance Information: Batch #S13PK8: For Further Information contact Rosen Publishing, New York, New York at 1-800-237-9932

# CONTENTS

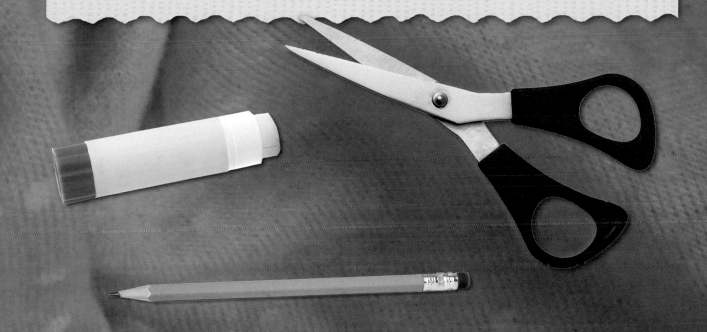

# DESIGNER WASTE?

When people talk about **recycling** waste instead of throwing it in the garbage, they are usually talking about items such as plastic bottles, glass jars, or old magazines. But how about recycling old clothes and other **textiles**?

About five percent of the waste that ends up in **landfills** in the United States each year is textiles and footwear. In fact, enough of these items are thrown away annually, that it amounts to 68 pounds (31 kg) of waste, or over 200 items of clothing, for every person in the United States!

Unwanted clothes don't have to be thrown out. One way to give them a second life is to give them to a **charity** that will sell the clothes to raise funds for their work. Another way to give old, damaged, or unwanted clothes a new life is to recycle them and make them into something completely new!

Coats, jackets, shirts, sweaters, jeans, underwear, socks, hats, scarves, bags, sheets, blankets, curtains, bath towels, tablecloths, and even dish towels can all be reused or recycled.

You can give your unwanted clothes to a thrift shop. Many charities raise funds by selling items in thrift shops.

YES
PLEASE

✓ CLOTHIN
✓ TOWELS
✓ SHEETS
✓ BLANKET
✓ SHOES
✓ CURTAIN

**CLOTHING BANK**

Look for textile recycling drop-off boxes in your neighborhood. The textiles are collected and sent to factories where the materials are recycled into products as varied as paper and construction materials.

# RECYCLED JEANS BAG

They've been your absolute favorites for ages, but now your jeans with the shredded knees are headed for the garbage.

That's a real shame, because around 950 gallons (3596 l) of water were used to grow the **cotton** and to manufacture the denim fabric in those jeans. Energy was used to make the denim, stitch the jeans, and transport them from a factory, to a store, and finally to your home.

A lot of precious **natural resources** went into making your jeans, so how about recycling them and turning them into a fantastic tote bag? You can also recycle one of your dad's old neckties to make a funky handle for the bag!

## You will need:

- A pair of old denim jeans
- Scissors
- Pins
- Blue cotton
- Needle
- Necktie
- Brooch or pin

## STEP 1:

Cut off the legs of the jeans about 1 inch (2.5 cm) below the bottom of the back pockets. Keep the legs to reuse in another denim project in the future.

## STEP 2:

Cut out the center seam. Then cut off any thick seams where the legs, front, and back of the jeans join up.

7

## STEP 3:

Turn the jeans inside out, flatten them, and line up the two sides—the jeans will now look a little like a short skirt.

Pin line

## STEP 4:

Pin the two sides together using a line of pins. Wherever you make the pin line will be the bottom the bag.

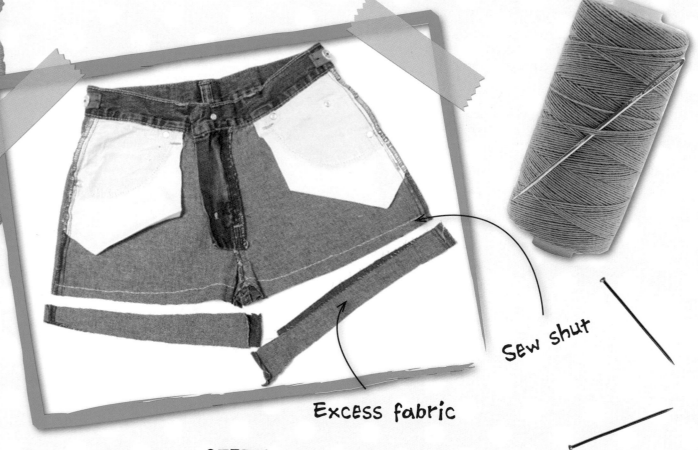

Sew shut

Excess fabric

## STEP 5:

Now sew along the pin line to close up the bottom of the bag. Be sure to remove the pins when you're done! Trim off the excess fabric.

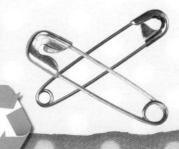

## STEP 6:

Turn the bag right side out, and it's ready to decorate.

## STEP 7:

Thread the necktie through the belt loops to make the bag's handle as shown. Securely pin the two ends of the necktie to the jeans with a brooch.

# FABRIC-COVERED JOURNAL

Using a piece of unwanted fabric, you can turn a worn-out ring binder into a unique, fabric-covered **journal**.

This project combines recycling fabric scraps (perhaps the leftover fabric from making the denim tote bag on page 6) with paper recycling. Every ton (t) of paper that is recycled saves huge quantities of resources needed to produce new paper. In fact, it saves 17 trees, 7,000 gallons (26,500 l) of water, and the amount of electricity used in an average American home during five months.

To make your journal, collect fabric scraps, buttons, beads, and paper scraps. You can also recycle printer paper that's only been used on one side and use the clean side as a place to record your thoughts, secrets, and dreams.

## You will need:

- A ring binder
- A piece of fabric large enough to cover the binder
- A glue gun
- Fabric scraps, buttons, beads, and any other recycled decorative items
- A length of ribbon (long enough to wind around the closed binder two times)
- Recycled paper
- A hole punch

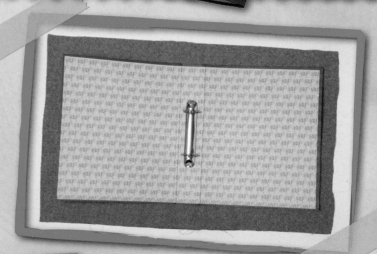

**STEP 1:**
Trim the piece of fabric so it is about 1 inch (2.5 cm) larger than the open binder.

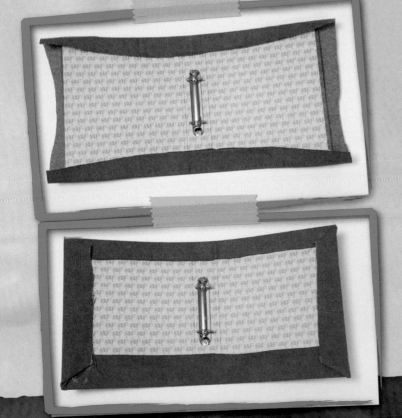

**STEP 2:**
Carefully squeeze some hot glue onto the inside of the binder's spine, top, and bottom. Then neatly fold over the fabric and press onto the glue. Continue to squeeze glue around the edge of the binder, then fold in the fabric and press onto the glue. Neatly fold in the corners—a little like when you are wrapping a gift.

11

## STEP 3:
Glue pieces of fabric or thick paper into the binder to make the insides of the binder look neat.

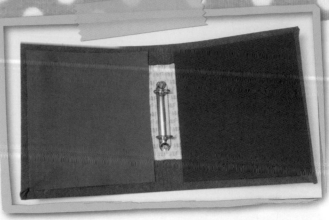

## STEP 4:
Now, create your design for the journal's cover. Try out different ideas with fabric scraps and decorations before gluing them onto the cover.

## STEP 5:
Collect paper for the inside of the journal. Use paper scraps of all sizes and colors. You can even insert pieces of gift wrap paper to add extra color.

## STEP 6:
Use a hole punch to make holes in the paper, and arrange the pieces of paper inside the journal.

**STEP 7:**

Glue a large bead close to the open edge of the front cover. Tie the ribbon around the bead, and then wrap the ribbon around the journal to keep all your secrets safe inside!

Wrap the ribbon around the journal to keep it shut.

Tie the ribbon around a large bead.

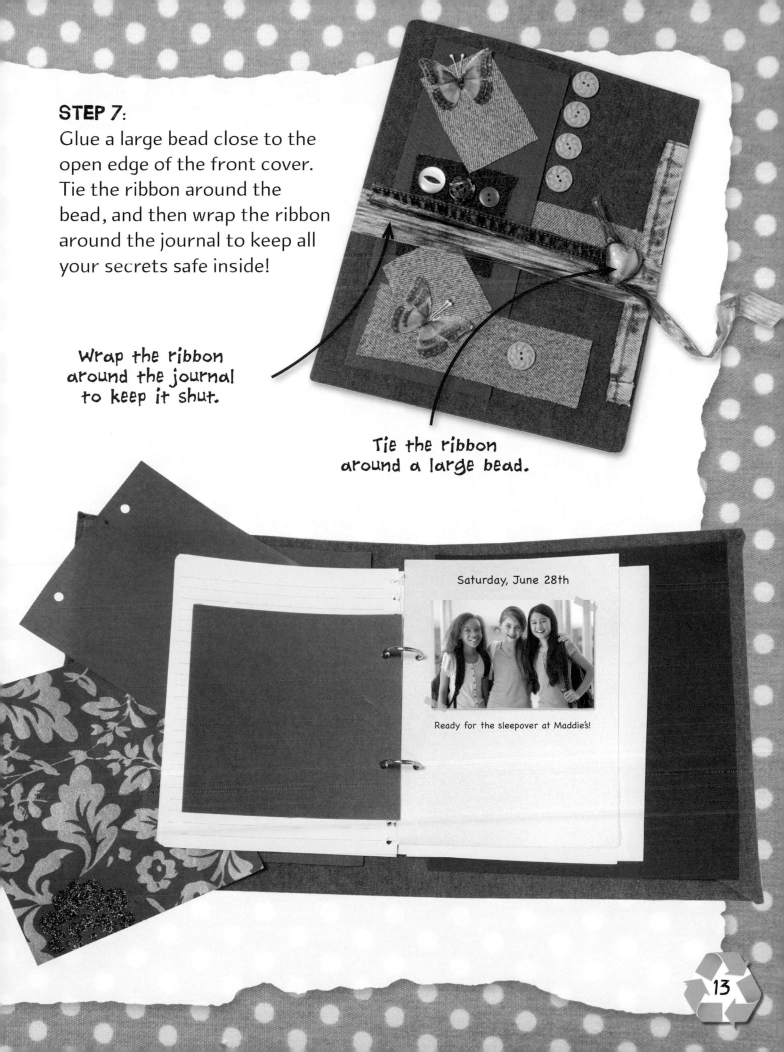

Saturday, June 28th

Ready for the sleepover at Maddie's!

# FABRIC SCRAP BOWLS

**When unwanted clothes and other textiles are sent to a recycling center, they can be made into many new products.**

Some fabrics get new lives as wiping or polishing cloths. Wool clothing can be turned into material for stuffing car seats or sofas. And because cotton is a natural product that comes from plants, it can sometimes be recycled into an ingredient in the **compost** that people use for growing plants.

You can recycle your old clothes and other fabric scraps by turning them into these pretty bowls. They make great gifts and can be used for holding jewelry and make-up, or for keeping a desk organized.

## You will need:
- Fabric scraps
- Scissors
- A ceramic or plastic bowl
- Plastic wrap
- White glue (mixed three parts glue to one part water)
- A paintbrush

**STEP 1:**
Cut the fabric into thin strips or small squares.

**STEP 2:**
Choose a ceramic or plastic bowl that will be the form, or shape, for your bowl. Cover the bowl with plastic wrap.

## STEP 3:
Using the paintbrush, paint some glue onto the upturned bowl. Then lay a piece of fabric onto the glue and paint more glue over the fabric.

## STEP 4:
Repeat step 3 with more pieces of fabric. Position some pieces so that they will form an edge, or rim, to the bowl.

## STEP 5:
Keep adding pieces of fabric until the bowl is completely covered. Make sure that all the fabric has been painted with glue. Don't worry if the glue looks white. It will be see-through when it dries. Leave the bowl to dry for 24 hours.

## STEP 6:

When the fabric bowl is dry and hard, carefully peel the plastic wrap from the ceramic or plastic bowl. The fabric bowl will come off, too. Gently remove the plastic wrap from the fabric bowl.

## STEP 7:

The rim of the fabric bowl will have rough edges, so carefully trim around the bowl to create a neat, smooth rim. Your fabric scraps bowl is ready to use!

Trim off these rough edges.

# SWEATER CUSHION

This next project shows you how to make a cushion cover from an unwanted button-down sweater. You can even stuff the cushion with old, but clean, socks and tights!

When tights and socks get holes or runs, they mostly end up in landfills, contributing to the millions of tons (t) of textiles that are simply buried in the ground each year. And because tights are made of **synthetic** fabrics, it may take these items hundreds of years to break down, or rot.

So do your part to keep sweaters, tights, and old socks out of landfills by turning them into colorful, cozy cushions!

## You will need:

- An old or unwanted cardigan (button-down sweater)
- Scissors
- Pins
- A needle and thread
- A pillowcase
- Old socks and tights

**STEP 1:**

Begin by taking a good look at the sweater and decide how the design could be used to make a cushion cover.

Collar trim

For example, you could cut off the top section and the arms of the sweater. Then cut off the trim around the collar to decorate the top edge of the cushion.

## STEP 2:

Pin and then stitch up the bottom of the sweater. Then pin and stitch up the top, cut edge of the sweater. Next, pin and stitch the collar trim to the top edge and stitch on a fifth button from the top part of the sweater that was discarded.

## STEP 3:

To make a cushion to go inside the cushion cover, take an old or unwanted pillowcase. In one corner mark out the size of your cushion cover. If you use a corner of the pillow case, two sides of your cushion will already be sewn up.

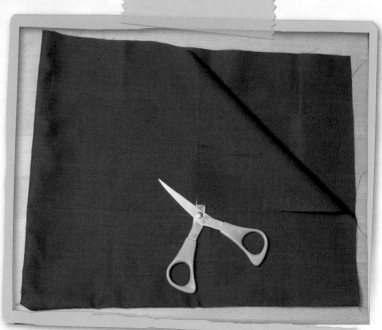

## STEP 4:

To make the stuffing to go inside the cushion, cut old socks and tights into small pieces. You can also cut up any unwanted pieces of the sweater, or save these for a different recycling project!

## STEP 5:

Sew up one of the open sides of the cushion that you've cut from the pillow case. Then stuff the cushion with the pieces of socks and tights, and sew up the fourth side.

## STEP 6:

Finally unbutton the cushion cover and insert the cushion.

Always save small fabric scraps as stuffing for cushions or soft toys.

# FUNKY FABRIC STORAGE JARS

Every month in the United States, enough glass jars and bottles are thrown away to fill a massive skyscraper.

If those jars and bottles end up in landfills, it's been estimated they will take more than 4,000 years to **decompose**. So reusing glass jars in craft projects is a great way to be **environmentally friendly**.

Unwanted pieces of fabric can be used to decorate recycled glass jars to make fun containers for storing cookies, coins, and other small items. These jars also make unique, green gifts!

22

## You will need:
- Clean, empty glass jars with lids
- Fabric scraps
- A marker
- Saucers, cups, or drinking glasses
- Scissors
- A glue gun
- Buttons
- Pieces of ribbon

## STEP 1:
Depending on the size of the jar's lid, draw around a saucer, cup, or glass to make a circle shape on a piece of fabric. The circle should be large enough to cover the sides of the lid.

## STEP 2:
Cut out the circle shape from the fabric. You can save the fabric scraps for future projects!

## STEP 3:
Cover the top of the lid with glue and press the lid down in the center of the fabric circle.

## STEP 4:
Squeeze dots of glue onto the side of the lid. Fold up the fabric and press into the glue, while slightly pleating the fabric.

**STEP 5:**
To decorate the jar, cut shapes from pieces of fabric.

**STEP 6:**
Glue the shapes to the sides of the jar.

**STEP 7:**
Finally, glue on buttons or add a piece of ribbon tied in a bow to the jar's lid. Be as creative as you want!

25

# T-SHIRT BRACELETS

You've probably heard people say that we live in a disposable society. This means that things people might once have used for a long time, or repaired when they got old or damaged, are now so cheap, it's possible to just throw them away and buy new ones!

In the world of fashion, one example of this is T-shirts. Today, it's possible to buy a cotton T-shirt for less than a cup of coffee. And yet to grow enough cotton to make a T-shirt, 700 gallons (2,650 l) of precious water are used. So once you're tired of a T-shirt, or it has become too worn out to wear, recycle it and give it a second life by turning the fabric into some cool bracelets and bangles.

## You will need:

- Two T-shirts in contrasting colors
- Scissors
- Bangles

**STEP 1:**
Starting at the bottom hem of a T-shirt, cut off a strip that's about 1 inch (2.5 cm) wide and about 24 inches (60 cm) long.

**STEP 2:**
Keep cutting until you've turned the body of the T-shirt into strips. Repeat with another T-shirt that's a contrasting color.

**STEP 3:**
Gently pull on the strips of fabric to stretch them, and they will curl up and look like thick yarn.

**STEP 4:**
Take three strips and tie them together.

**STEP 5:**
Now braid the strips together.

**STEP 6:**

Once you've made a braid long enough for a bracelet, tie up the strands so the braid doesn't unravel, and then tie the two ends of the bracelet together. You can join the two ends by tying a strand from each end together into a double knot. Trim off any excess fabric.

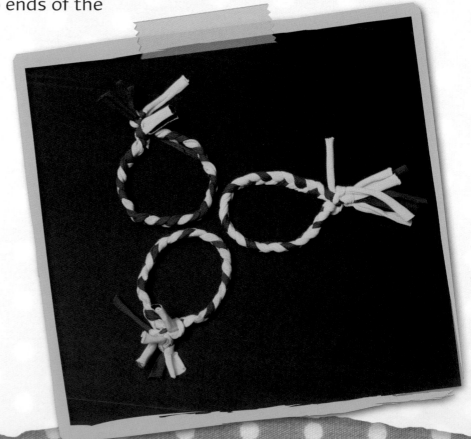

## STEP 7:

To make a bangle, tie a strand of T-shirt fabric onto an old or unwanted bangle.

## STEP 8:

Tightly wrap the fabric strand around the bangle. When the whole bangle is covered with fabric, tie the two ends of the strand tightly together and trim off any excess.

# GLOSSARY

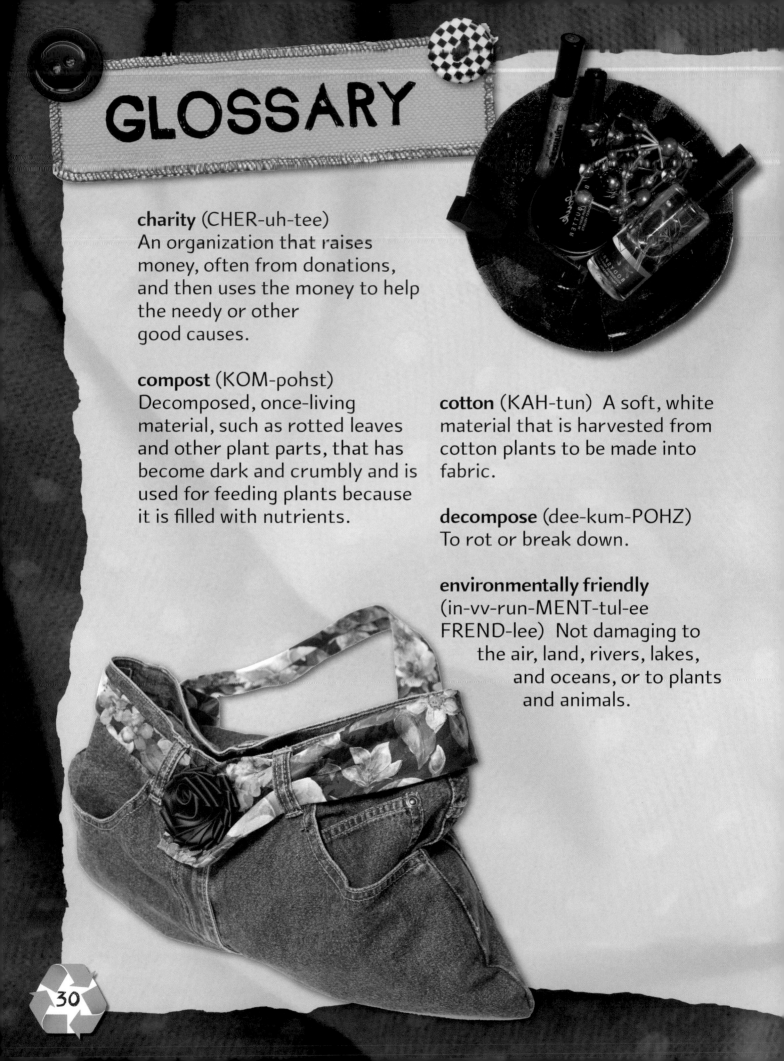

**charity** (CHER-uh-tee)
An organization that raises money, often from donations, and then uses the money to help the needy or other good causes.

**compost** (KOM-pohst)
Decomposed, once-living material, such as rotted leaves and other plant parts, that has become dark and crumbly and is used for feeding plants because it is filled with nutrients.

**cotton** (KAH-tun) A soft, white material that is harvested from cotton plants to be made into fabric.

**decompose** (dee-kum-POHZ)
To rot or break down.

**environmentally friendly**
(in-vv-run-MENT-tul-ee FREND-lee) Not damaging to the air, land, rivers, lakes, and oceans, or to plants and animals.

**journal** (JER-nul) A notebook in which a person writes down his or her thoughts or experiences; a diary.

**landfills** (LAND-filz) A large site where garbage is dumped and buried.

**natural resources**
(NA-chuh-rul REE-sors-ez) Materials or substances that occur in nature such as wood, rocks, and water.

**recycling** (ree-SY-kling) Turning used materials into new products.

**synthetic** (sin-THEH-tik) A material or substance that does not occur naturally but has been made by people.

**textiles** (TEK-stylz) Fabrics such as cotton, denim, and silk.

# WEBSITES

Due to the changing nature of Internet links, PowerKids Press has developed an online list of websites related to the subject of this book. This site is updated regularly. Please use this link to access the list:

www.powerkidslinks.com/ftt/fabric/

# READ MORE

**Green, Jen**. *Why Should I Recycle?* Why Should I? Hauppauge, NY: Barron's Educational Series, 2005.

**Lim, Annalees**. *Fun with Fabric*. Clever Crafts. New York: Windmill Books, 2013.

**Ridley, Sarah**. *A Cotton T-Shirt*. How It's Made. New York: Gareth Stevens Learning Library, 2006.

# INDEX